Contents

How to use this book ...

Fractions   3-4

Mixed fractions   5-6

Equivalent fractions   7-8

Fractions   9

Percentages   10-16

Multiples   17-20

Square numbers   21

Square roots   22

Factors   23-25

Dividing rules   26-28

Solving equations   29-30

Subtraction   31-36

Dividing   37-46

Solving problems   47-49

Multiplying decimals   50-57

Dividing   58-61

Dividing decimals   62-64

KU-351-009

How to use this book

Each page has a title telling you what it is about.

Instructions look like this. Always read these carefully before starting.

Sometimes there is a 'Hint' to help you.

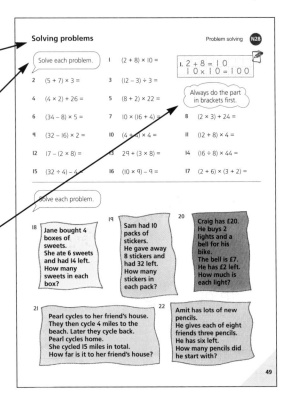

This shows you how to set out your work. The first question is usually done for you.

Sometimes you need materials to help you with the activity.

This shows that the activity is an 'Explore'. Work with a friend.

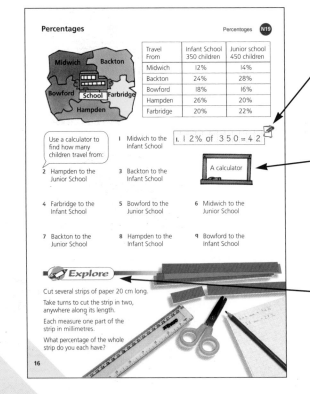

Fractions

Copy each grid and colour the fraction shown.

1   $\frac{1}{4}$

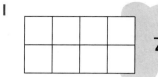

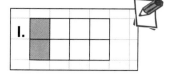

I.

2   $\frac{1}{5}$

3   $\frac{3}{4}$

4   $\frac{1}{2}$

5   $\frac{2}{3}$

6   $\frac{1}{4}$

7   $\frac{3}{10}$

Write the fraction of each shape that is blue.

8

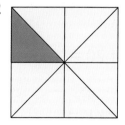

8. $\frac{1}{4}$

9

10

11

12

13

14

Write the fraction of each shape that is yellow.

8a. $\frac{3}{4}$

3

Fractions

Write what fraction of each set is red.

1

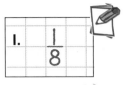

1. $\frac{1}{8}$

2

3

4

5

6

7

Copy and complete.

8 $\frac{1}{4}$ of 24 =

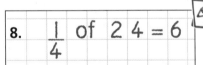

8. $\frac{1}{4}$ of 2 4 = 6

9 $\frac{1}{3}$ of 9 =

10 $\frac{1}{2}$ of 14 =

11 $\frac{1}{6}$ of 36 =

12 $\frac{1}{8}$ of 24 =

13 $\frac{2}{3}$ of 12 =

14 $\frac{3}{4}$ of 48 =

15 $\frac{5}{6}$ of 30 =

16 $\frac{2}{5}$ of 15 =

17 $\frac{5}{9}$ of 18 =

18 $\frac{3}{4}$ of 80 =

19 $\frac{1}{2}$ of 80 =

20 $\frac{1}{5}$ of 20 =

21 $\frac{1}{6}$ of 24 =

22 $\frac{2}{3}$ of 90 =

23 $\frac{1}{12}$ of 48 =

24 $\frac{5}{8}$ of 40 =

25 $\frac{1}{3}$ of 33 =

26 $\frac{3}{5}$ of 30 =

Mixed fractions

Write how many straws in each set.

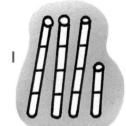

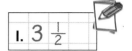

1. $3\frac{1}{2}$

2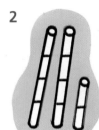

3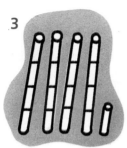

4

5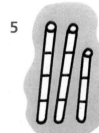

6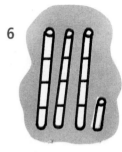

Write how many cakes in each set.

7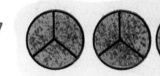

7. $2\frac{2}{3}$

8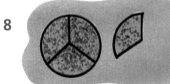

9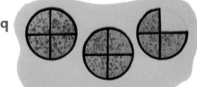

10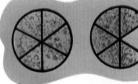

11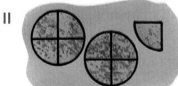

12

13

14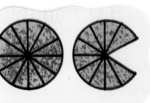

15

16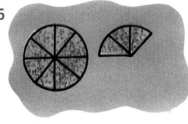

Draw cakes to match these fractions.

17 $1\frac{2}{3}$

17.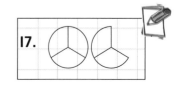

18 $2\frac{3}{4}$ **19** $1\frac{5}{8}$ **20** $2\frac{1}{3}$ **21** $3\frac{1}{4}$

Mixed fractions

Write how many bars of chocolate in each set.

1. $2\frac{3}{8}$

1

2

3

4

5

6

7

8

9

10

Write the length of each flight in minutes.

11. $1\frac{1}{2}$ hours $= 90$ minutes

11
Paris
$1\frac{1}{2}$ hours

12
Amsterdam
$1\frac{1}{4}$ hours

13
Madrid
$3\frac{1}{4}$ hours

14
Bonn
$2\frac{1}{3}$ hours

15
Dublin
$\frac{3}{4}$ hour

16
Berlin
$2\frac{5}{6}$ hours

17
Oslo
$2\frac{1}{4}$ hours

18
North Pole
$3\frac{3}{4}$ hours

Equivalent fractions

Write the pairs of fractions that match.

a

c

d

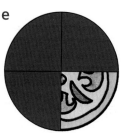
e

b

1. a and g
$$\frac{3}{4} = \frac{6}{8}$$

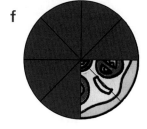

g

h

f

i

j

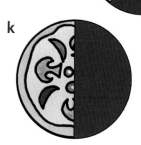
k

l

Write the missing numbers.

7 $\frac{2}{3} = \frac{}{6}$

7. $\frac{2}{3} = \frac{4}{6}$

8 $\frac{3}{5} = \frac{}{10}$

9 $\frac{3}{} = \frac{9}{12}$

10 $\frac{}{2} = \frac{6}{12}$

11 $\frac{5}{8} = \frac{10}{}$

12 $\frac{4}{} = \frac{1}{3}$

13 $\frac{3}{4} = \frac{}{16}$

14 $\frac{2}{} = \frac{6}{9}$

15 $\frac{1}{6} = \frac{}{12}$

16 $\frac{1}{4} = \frac{4}{}$

17 $\frac{1}{2} = \frac{}{10}$

18 $\frac{8}{10} = \frac{}{5}$

19 $\frac{2}{4} = \frac{}{8}$

7

Equivalent fractions

Write each fraction in its simplest form.

1 $\dfrac{4}{16}$

I. $\dfrac{4}{16} = \dfrac{1}{4}$

1	2	3	4	5	6	7	8	9	10
2	4	6	8	10	12	14	16	18	20
3	6	9	12	15	18	21	24	27	30
4	8	12	16	20	24	28	32	36	40
5	10	15	20	25	30	35	40	45	50
6	12	18	24	30	36	42	48	54	60
7	14	21	28	35	42	49	56	63	70
8	16	24	32	40	48	56	64	72	80
9	18	27	36	45	54	63	72	81	90
10	20	30	40	50	60	70	80	90	100

2 $\dfrac{15}{20}$ 　 3 $\dfrac{5}{10}$ 　 4 $\dfrac{6}{14}$

5 $\dfrac{5}{15}$ 　 6 $\dfrac{3}{24}$ 　 7 $\dfrac{10}{30}$

8 $\dfrac{8}{12}$ 　 9 $\dfrac{8}{20}$ 　 10 $\dfrac{30}{42}$

Write 2 other fractions equivalent to each.

Ia. $\dfrac{4}{16} = \dfrac{5}{20} = \dfrac{7}{28}$

Write 3 other fractions equivalent to each.

11 $\dfrac{1}{2}$

II. $\dfrac{1}{2} = \dfrac{3}{6} = \dfrac{5}{10} = \dfrac{9}{18}$

12 $\dfrac{1}{4}$ 　 13 $\dfrac{1}{5}$ 　 14 $\dfrac{2}{3}$ 　 15 $\dfrac{3}{4}$ 　 16 $\dfrac{1}{6}$

17 $\dfrac{1}{10}$ 　 18 $\dfrac{1}{7}$ 　 19 $\dfrac{2}{5}$ 　 20 $\dfrac{3}{8}$ 　 21 $\dfrac{1}{9}$

Fractions

Write $<\frac{1}{2}$, $>\frac{1}{2}$ or $=\frac{1}{2}$ for each.

1 $\frac{2}{4}$

1. $\frac{2}{4} = \frac{1}{2}$

2 $\frac{1}{3}$

3 $\frac{3}{5}$

4 $\frac{2}{7}$

5 $\frac{8}{16}$

6 $\frac{5}{10}$

7 $\frac{10}{30}$

8 $\frac{5}{20}$

9 $\frac{2}{3}$

10 $\frac{9}{12}$

11 $\frac{5}{8}$

Write $<$, $>$ or $=$ between each pair.

12 $\frac{1}{4}$ $\frac{4}{8}$

12. $\frac{1}{4} < \frac{4}{8}$

13 $\frac{1}{3}$ $\frac{2}{6}$

14 $\frac{1}{5}$ $\frac{2}{10}$

15 $\frac{1}{6}$ $\frac{6}{18}$

16 $\frac{3}{4}$ $\frac{8}{12}$

17 $\frac{2}{5}$ $\frac{4}{10}$

18 $\frac{1}{9}$ $\frac{6}{54}$

19 $\frac{2}{7}$ $\frac{6}{14}$

20 $\frac{1}{10}$ $\frac{4}{40}$

21 $\frac{1}{2}$ $\frac{11}{20}$

22 $\frac{2}{5}$ $\frac{3}{10}$

Explore

Use number cards 1 to 10.

Use 2 cards to make a fraction – the top card must be smaller than the bottom card.

Investigate fractions that are less than, more than or equal to one half.

1

4

$\frac{1}{3} < \frac{1}{2}$

$\frac{1}{4} < \frac{1}{2}$

Percentages

Write what percentage of each grid is blue.

1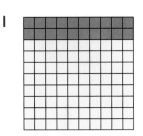

1. 2 0 %

2 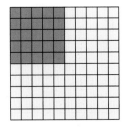 3 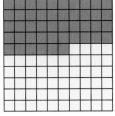 4 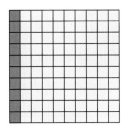 5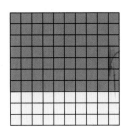

6 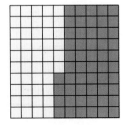 7 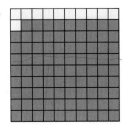 8 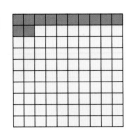 9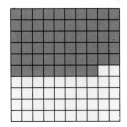

Write what percentage of each grid is yellow.

1a. 8 0 %

Draw 10 × 10 grids and colour each percentage.

10 15%

11 29%

12 1%

13 50%

14 5%

15 7%

16 82%

17 68%

Write each percentage as a decimal.

10a. 0·15

10

Percentages

Write each fraction as a percentage.

1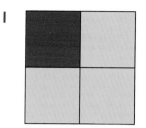

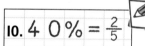
1. $\frac{1}{4} = 25\%$

2

3

4

5

6

7

8

q

Write each percentage as a fraction in its simplest form.

10   40%

10. $40\% = \frac{2}{5}$

11   30%   12   20%   13   5%   14   10%   15   50%

16   75%   17   80%   18   70%   19   35%   20   90%

Write each decimal as a percentage.

21   0·16

21. $0·16 = 16\%$

22   0·73   23   0·4   24   0·66   25   0·04   26   0·17

27   0·08   28   0·54   29   0·2   30   0·23   31   0·99

Percentages

Write the missing numbers.

1   $25\% = \dfrac{1}{\ }$

1. $25\% = \dfrac{1}{4}$

2   $0.3 = \dfrac{\ }{10}$

3   $\dfrac{12}{\ } = 12\%$

4   $\dfrac{73}{\ } = 0.73$

5   $\dfrac{2}{\ } = 20\%$

6   $54\% = \dfrac{\ }{100}$

7   $\dfrac{14}{100} = 0.\ $

8   $\dfrac{1}{5} = \ \%$

9   $0.18 = \dfrac{\ }{100}$

10   $50\% = \dfrac{5}{\ }$

Write <, > or $\doteq$ between each pair.

11   75% 0.68

11. $75\% > 0.68$

12   0.71 $\dfrac{17}{100}$

13   0.36 $\dfrac{36}{100}$

14   85% 0.85

15   $\dfrac{27}{100}$ 30%

16   55% $\dfrac{44}{100}$

17   31% 0.13

18   21% $\dfrac{21}{100}$

19   0.43 $\dfrac{44}{100}$

20   8% $\dfrac{80}{100}$

Write each set in order from smallest to largest.

21   0.27 50% $\dfrac{35}{100}$

21. $0.27, \dfrac{35}{100}, 50\%$

22

0.75 $\dfrac{70}{100}$ 71%

23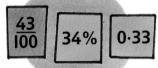

$\dfrac{43}{100}$ 34% 0.33

24

0.18 $\dfrac{81}{100}$ 8%

25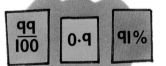

$\dfrac{99}{100}$ 0.9 91%

26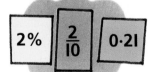

2% $\dfrac{2}{10}$ 0.21

27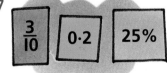

$\dfrac{3}{10}$ 0.2 25%

Percentages

> 50% of the people at each film are children.

> Write how many children.

1. 8 0 children

1
160 people

2
360 people

3
184 people

4
448 people

5
140 people

6
240 people

7
336 people

8
264 people

> 25% of people didn't like the film.

> Write how many people.

1a. 4 0 people

> Write 10% of each amount.

9
£60

9. 1 0% of £ 6 0 = £ 6

10 £120

11 £560

12 £380

13 £990

14 £1070

15 £2200

16 £6010

17 £10

Percentages

Write how many children voted 'yes' in each school.

I PARK ROAD
140 children
20% voted yes

1. 10% of $140 = 14$
   20% of $140 = 28$

2 ST JOHNS
280 children
30% voted yes

3 ROSETREE
190 children
40% voted yes

4 HOLY CROSS
250 children
50% voted yes

5 CASTLE HILL
360 children
10% voted yes

6 MID VALE
180 children
30% voted yes

7 SANDY LANE
340 children
20% voted yes

8 GREENFIELD
170 children
40% voted yes

q WOODGREEN
220 children
60% voted yes

Copy and complete.

10 80% of 200 =

10. 10% of $200 = 20$
    80% of $200 = 160$

II 30% of 120 =

12 40% of 40 =

13 20% of 350 =

14 50% of 36 =

15 10% of 400 =

16 30% of 300 =

17 70% of 200 =

18 20% of 150 =

19 90% of 500 =

20 60% of 600 =

21 40% of 250 =

22 50% of 70 =

Percentages

> 10% of the flowers in each survey were blue.

> Write how many flowers in total.

I. 3 6 0

1
36 blue flowers

2
24 blue flowers

3
10 blue flowers

4
6 blue flowers

5
18 blue flowers

6
30 blue flowers

7
4 blue flowers

8
19 blue flowers

9
11 blue flowers

10
1 blue flower

11
22 blue flowers

12
8 blue flowers

> Each price goes down by 10%.

> Write the new price.

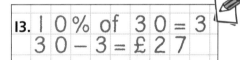

13. 1 0 % of 3 0 = 3
3 0 − 3 = £ 2 7

13
£30

14
£50

15
£20

16
£100

17
£90

18
£110

19
£80

20
£40

21
£60

Percentages

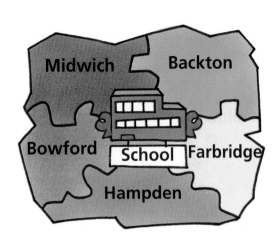

Travel From	Infant School 350 children	Junior school 450 children
Midwich	12%	14%
Backton	24%	28%
Bowford	18%	16%
Hampden	26%	20%
Farbridge	20%	22%

> Use a calculator to find how many children travel from:

1 Midwich to the Infant School

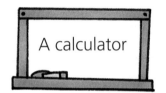

1. 12% of $350 = 42$

A calculator

2 Hampden to the Junior School

3 Backton to the Infant School

4 Farbridge to the Infant School

5 Bowford to the Junior School

6 Midwich to the Junior School

7 Backton to the Junior School

8 Hampden to the Infant School

9 Bowford to the Infant School

Explore

Cut several strips of paper 20 cm long.

Take turns to cut the strip in two, anywhere along its length.

Each measure one part of the strip in millimetres.

What percentage of the whole strip do you each have?

Multiples

Write the missing multiples.

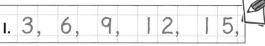

1. 3, 6, 9, 12, 15,

1 3   6   9   21

2 12   16   20   32

3 21   28   42   56

4 20   25   30

5 9   18   72

6 24   30   36

7 16   32   48   72

8 12   18   36

Write the:

9 3rd multiple of 6

9. 18

10 7th multiple of 2

11 4th multiple of 7

12 9th multiple of 3

13 6th multiple of 6

14 10th multiple of 4

15 8th multiple of 5

16 5th multiple of 12

17 6th multiple of 30

18 3rd multiple of 15

19 2nd multiple of 20

20 3rd multiple of 11

21 5th multiple of 40

17

Multiples

> Copy and complete.

1. 9, 18, 27,

1   the multiples of 9   9   18   . . .   90

2   the multiples of 18   18   36   . . .   180

3   the multiples of 7   7   14   . . .   70

4   the multiples of 14   14   28   . . .   140

> Copy and complete.

5   $6 \times 18 =$

1. $6 \times 18 = 108$

6   $4 \times 14 =$ 7 $5 \times 18 =$ 8 $3 \times 18 =$ 9 $6 \times 14 =$

10   $4 \times 18 =$ 11 $7 \times 14 =$ 12 $5 \times 14 =$ 13 $3 \times 14 =$

> Write the next 5 multiples in each set.

14. 15, 30, 45, 60,

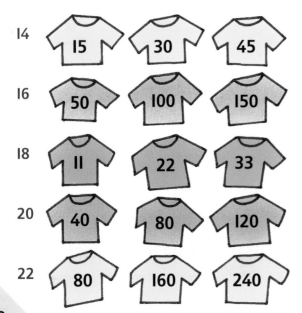

14   15   30   45

16   50   100   150

18   11   22   33

20   40   80   120

22   80   160   240

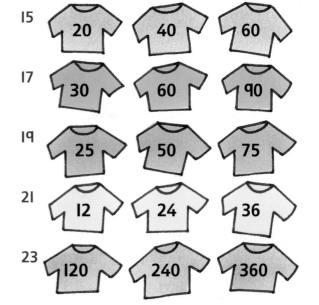

15   20   40   60

17   30   60   90

19   25   50   75

21   12   24   36

23   120   240   360

Multiples

> Write how many numbers from I to 50 are:

I	2	3	4	5	6	7	8	q	10
II	12	13	14	15	16	17	18	19	20
21	22	23	24	25	26	27	28	29	30
31	32	33	34	35	36	37	38	39	40
41	42	43	44	45	46	47	48	49	50

I **multiples of 2**    I. 2 5

2 **multiples of 3**

3 **multiples of 6**

4 **multiples of q**

5 **multiples of 7**

6 **multiples of both 3 and 4**

7 **multiples of both 5 and 6**

> Write each as a percentage.

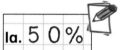 Ia. 5 0 %

24   q   18   15   21   50   II   48   16   33   13   20

> Which of these are:

8 multiples of 3?   8. 2 4,   q,

q   multiples of 2 and 4?

10   odd multiples of 5?

II   even multiples of 3?

Explore

Use number cards 0 to q.

Use card '4' and one other to make multiples of different numbers.

Can you make multiples of all numbers from 2 to 10?

Try again using another card instead of 4.

Multiples

Write the first 4 multiples common to:

1	2	3	4	5	6	7	8	9	10
11	12	13	14	15	16	17	18	19	20
21	22	23	24	25	26	27	28	29	30
31	32	33	34	35	36	37	38	39	40
41	42	43	44	45	46	47	48	49	50
51	52	53	54	55	56	57	58	59	60
61	62	63	64	65	66	67	68	69	70
71	72	73	74	75	76	77	78	79	80
81	82	83	84	85	86	87	88	89	90
91	92	93	94	95	96	97	98	99	100

1 2 and 3   1. 6,   12,

2 2 and 4   **3** 3 and 4

4 3 and 5   **5** 2 and 5

6 3 and 7   **7** 4 and 6

8 4 and 5   **9** 5 and 6

10 2, 3 and 4   **11** 3, 4 and 6   **12** 2, 4 and 5

Write a number that is a multiple of:

13 2, 4 and 8   13. 16

14 2, 3 and 5   **15** 2, 4 and 6   **16** 1, 3 and 5

17 5, 10 and 20   **18** 3, 4 and 5   **19** 3, 5 and 6

20 3, 6 and 9   **21** 2, 6 and 8   **22** 2, 3 and 9

Write the smallest common multiple of each set.   13a. 8

Square numbers

Write how many pegs in each board.

1

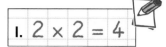

1. $2 \times 2 = 4$

2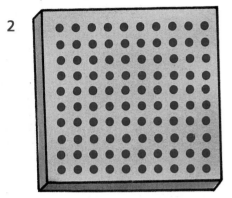

3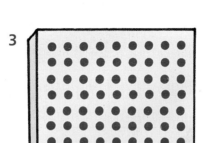

4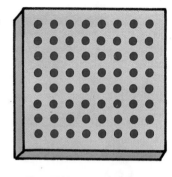

5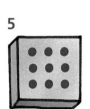

6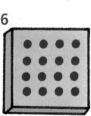

7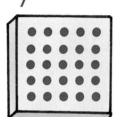

8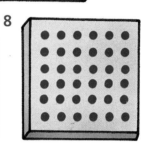

9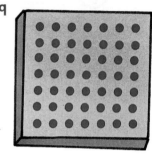

Write how many pegs would fit on a:

10   20 × 20 board

10. $20 \times 20 = 400$

11   30 × 30 board

12   40 × 40 board

13   50 × 50 board

14   15 × 15 board

Estimate the squares of these numbers.   Use a calculator to check.

15. estimate   → 400
     calculator → 441

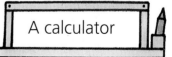

A calculator

15   **21**   16   **32**   17   **17**

18   **19**   19   **26**   20   **52**   21   **44**

22   **16**   23   **29**   24   **25**   25   **13**

Square roots

in	4	3	6
out	2		

Copy and complete the table.

in	4	36		81	16		100	9	49	
out			1			8				5

Estimate these square roots.

1 $\sqrt{10}$ 1. $\sqrt{10}$ → between 3 and 4

2 $\sqrt{20}$ 3 $\sqrt{70}$ 4 $\sqrt{5}$ 5 $\sqrt{60}$ 6 $\sqrt{90}$

7 $\sqrt{28}$ 8 $\sqrt{17}$ 9 $\sqrt{52}$ 10 $\sqrt{68}$ 11 $\sqrt{73}$

Use a calculator to find the square root of each number.

Write the first two decimal places only.

1a. $\sqrt{10} = 3.16$

Explore

Use a calculator to find some 3-digit numbers that have a whole number square root.

How many can you find less than 500?

$\sqrt{100} = 10$

$\sqrt{121} = 11$

Factors

> Write the missing numbers.

I. $10 = 1 \times 10, \quad 2 \times 5$

1 $\quad 10 = 1 \times$ ⬤ $, 2 \times$ ⬤

2 $\quad 14 = 1 \times$ ⬤ $, 2 \times$ ⬤

3 $\quad 16 = 1 \times$ ⬤ $, 2 \times$ ⬤ $, 4 \times$ ⬤

4 $\quad 21 = 1 \times$ ⬤ $, 3 \times$ ⬤

5 $\quad 35 = 1 \times$ ⬤ $, 5 \times$ ⬤

6 $\quad 48 = 1 \times$ ⬤ $, 2 \times$ ⬤ $, 3 \times$ ⬤ $, 4 \times$ ⬤ $, 6 \times$ ⬤

7 $\quad 42 = 1 \times$ ⬤ $, 2 \times$ ⬤ $, 3 \times$ ⬤ $, 6 \times$ ⬤

8 $\quad 60 = 1 \times$ ⬤ $, 2 \times$ ⬤ $, 3 \times$ ⬤ $, 4 \times$ ⬤ $, 5 \times$ ⬤ $, 6 \times$ ⬤

9 $\quad 25 = 1 \times$ ⬤ $, 5 \times$ ⬤

10 $\quad 18 = 1 \times$ ⬤ $, 2 \times$ ⬤ $, 3 \times$ ⬤

> List the factors of each number.

Ia. factors of 10: 1, 2, 5, 10

> Write all the different pairs of factors for these numbers.

II $\quad 12$

II. $1 \times 12, \quad 2 \times 6, \quad 3 \times 4$

12 24   **13** 32   **14** 36   **15** 28   **16** 30

17 40   **18** 45   **19** 50   **20** 23   **21** 49

> List the factors of each number.

IIa. factors of 12: 1, 2, 3, 4, 6, 12

Factors

Copy and complete this table to show the factors of numbers up to 40.

Number	Pairs of factors	List of factors
1	1 × 1	1
2	1 × 2	1, 2
3	1 × 3	1, 3
4	1 × 4, 2 × 2	1, 2, 4

Copy and complete this table to show how many factors each number has.

Describe any patterns you notice in the columns of this table.

Number of factors								
1	2	3	4	5	6	7	8	9
1	2	4	6					
	3	9	8					
	5							

 **Explore**

Draw a table with 6 columns and 10 rows.

Write the numbers 1 to 60 in order in the table.

Colour all the prime numbers.

Write about any patterns you notice.

1	2	3	4	5	6
7	8	9	10	11	12
13	14	15	16	17	18
19	20	21	22	23	24
25	26	27	28	29	30
31	32	33	34	35	36
37	38	39	40	41	42
43	44	45	46	47	48
49	50	51	52	53	54
55	56	57	58	59	60

Factors

60 can be split into 2 factors.

20 can be split into 2 factors.

4 can be split into 2 factors.

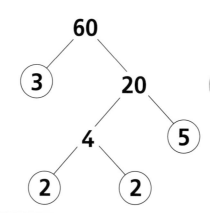

This is called a factor tree.

The circled numbers are prime.

Draw a factor tree for:

1	12	2	48	3	36
4	16	5	24	6	18

Which number from each list is not a factor of the star number?

7

24

8, 3, 6, 16

7. 1 6

8

36

3, 20, 12, 4

9

40

10, 4, 6, 2

10

50

2, 25, 15, 10

11

28

4, 6, 14, 7

12

32

2, 7, 16, 1

13

54

18, 7, 3, 2

14

56

14, 9, 7, 4

15

500

3, 10, 5, 2

Dividing rules

Find half of each number.

Write odd or even for each answer.

1. $6\ 4\ 8 \div 2 = 3\ 2\ 4$
$3\ 2\ 4\ \rightarrow\ $ even

1. **648**
2. **204**
3. **556**
4. **442**
5. **772**
6. **222**
7. **1004**
8. **906**
9. **7070**
10. **3422**
11. **6784**
12. **900**
13. **2002**
14. **9998**
15. **8886**
16. **6076**

Write which numbers divide by 2.

17. **344**

17. $3\ 4\ 4$ is even
$3\ 4\ 4$ divides by 2

18. **261**
19. **110**
20. **332**
21. **1002**
22. **710**
23. **881**
24. **1040**
25. **2000**
26. **201**
27. **1066**
28. **9096**
29. **792**
30. **4056**
31. **1666**
32. **1080**
33. **9090**
34. **4554**
35. **10 000**
36. **20 000**
37. **645**
38. **449**
39. **1036**
40. **2918**
41. **4040**

Write which numbers divide by 4.

17a. $3\ 4\ 4 \div 2 = 1\ 7\ 2$
$1\ 7\ 2$ is even
$3\ 4\ 4$ divides by 4

Dividing rules

Write which numbers divide by 5 and which divide by 10.

1
340

1.	3	4	0	divides by	5
	3	4	0	divides by	1 0

2
725

3
6005

4
500

5
75

6
6250

7
1000

8
225

9
1005

Write which numbers: divide by 2   divide by 4   divide by 5   divide by 10.

10
680

11
60

12
320

13
555

14
270

15
1000

16
900

17
305

18
999

19
348

20
770

21
504

10.	6 8 0	is even
	6 8 0	divides by	2

6 8 0 ÷ 2 = 3 4 0
3 4 0 is even
6 8 0 divides by 4

6 8 0 divides by 5

6 8 0 divides by 1 0

22
6060

23
7000

24
1515

25
1010

26
3300

27

Dividing rules

Write which numbers divide by 3.

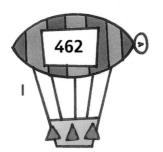

I. 462

I.
$4 + 6 + 2 = 12$
12 divides by 3
4 6 2 divides by 3

2 558

3 662

4 435

5 1008

6 990

7 738

8 444

9 6021

10 7398

II 9045

Write which numbers divide by 6.

Write which numbers divide by 9.

Ia.
4 6 2 divides by 3
4 6 2 is even
4 6 2 divides by 6

Copy and complete this table.

	÷ 2	÷ 3	÷ 4	÷ 5	÷ 6	÷ 9	÷ 10
60	✓	✓	✓	✓	✓	✗	✓
720							
945							
7644							
1000							
9000							

Solving equations

Solve these addition mysteries.

I $a + 3 = 5$

2 $b + 1 = 4$

3 $c + 3 = 8$

4 $d + 2 = 5$

5 $e + 4 = 6$

6 $3 + f = 9$

7 $6 + g = 10$

8 $12 = h + 1$

9 $9 = 4 + i$

10 $7 = j + 5$

II $8 = 1 + k$

I. $a + 3 = 5$
   $a = 2$

Solve these subtraction mysteries.

12 $7 - a = 2$

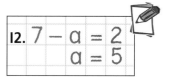

12. $7 - a = 2$
    $a = 5$

13 $10 - b = 4$

14 $9 - c = 7$

15 $8 - d = 1$

16 $13 - e = 5$

17 $f - 6 = 8$

18 $g - 1 = 3$

19 $h - 7 = 7$

20 $12 = i - 4$

21 $13 - j = 6$

22 $9 = k - 2$

29

Solving equations

Solve these mysteries.

1 $a + 39 = 47$

1. $a + 39 = 47$
$a = 8$

2 $b + 25 = 29$ **3** $c + 34 = 35$ **4** $15 + d = 18$

5 $46 + x = 49$ **6** $25 - y = 22$ **7** $34 - h = 30$

8 $y - 13 = 14$ **9** $m + 21 = 38 - 2$ **10** $48 - p = 16 + 3$

11 $12 + q = 45 - 30$ **12** $29 - n = 12 + 5$ **13** $15 + 21 = 47 - s$

Match each equation to its card.

14 $3 + q = 8$

14. $3 + q = 8$
$q = 5$

15 $q + 4 = 8$ **16** $q - 2 = 4$ **17** $5 - q = 3$ **18** $2 = q + 1$

19 $4 = q - 3$ **20** $6 = 15 - q$ **21** $7 = 4 + q$ **22** $q + 5 = 10$

Which card is not matched?

Solve these mysteries.

23 $4 \times m = 12$

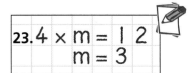

23. $4 \times m = 12$
$m = 3$

24 $d \times 7 = 42$ **25** $25 = 5 \times z$ **26** $56 = p \times 7$ **27** $81 = 9 \times q$

28 $g = 6 \times 6$ **29** $56 = 4 \times p$ **30** $6 \times h = 42$ **31** $2 \times k = 32$

Add to each to make the next hundred, then the next thousand.

1

4642

1. $4642 + 58 = 4700$
$4700 + 300 = 5000$

2
3543

3
2748

4
5489

5
6666

6
7207

7
4098

8
8974

9
2323

10
6540

11
5044

12
9777

13
1691

Copy and complete.

14.

$+16$

```
  7 4 7 2
− 3 5 8 4
```

$+400$

```
  7 4 8 8
− 3 6 0 0
```

```
  7 8 8 8
− 4 0 0 0
  3 8 8 8
```

14
```
  7 4 7 2
− 3 5 8 4
```

15
```
  5 7 4 3
− 3 8 2 9
```

16
```
  7 0 1 3
− 2 1 3 4
```

17
```
  4 6 2 0
− 3 7 4 4
```

18
```
  5 8 1 7
− 2 9 8 2
```

19
```
  6 3 1 2
− 3 6 6 7
```

20
```
  9 0 4 3
− 3 8 3 8
```

21
```
  6 4 1 2
− 4 6 2 1
```

Copy and complete.

1.
```
  6 8 5 2
- 4 2 2 8
─────────
```

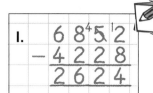

1.
```
  6 8⁴5¹2
- 4 2 2 8
─────────
  2 6 2 4
```

2.
```
  4 3 8 1
- 2 1 6 7
─────────
```

3.
```
  5 5 5 5
- 2 3 4 8
─────────
```

4.
```
  7 6 4 1
- 2 4 3 3
─────────
```

5.
```
  6 8 2 0
- 1 4 7 1
─────────
```

6.
```
  8 4 3 5
- 6 4 1 6
─────────
```

7.
```
  9 3 8 4
- 7 2 2 8
─────────
```

8.
```
  6 4 2 8
- 4 1 1 9
─────────
```

9.
```
  5 8 7 3
- 2 4 6 6
─────────
```

Copy and complete.

10.
```
  4 3 2 3
- 1 2 4 8
─────────
```

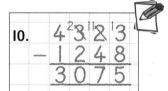

10.
```
  4²3¹1²3
- 1 2 4 8
─────────
  3 0 7 5
```

11.
```
  6 4 2 1
- 4 2 8 8
─────────
```

12.
```
  7 4 3 4
- 5 2 7 5
─────────
```

13.
```
  8 2 5 3
- 6 4 2 5
─────────
```

14.
```
  5 2 7 1
- 3 4 8 2
─────────
```

15.
```
  9 3 0 2
- 5 2 9 7
─────────
```

16.
```
  8 7 1 1
- 1 8 6 6
─────────
```

17.
```
  6 0 2 3
- 3 7 6 5
─────────
```

18.
```
  7 5 2 7
- 1 3 8 8
─────────
```

Taking away

Find the difference in price between each pair of cars.

B

£9611

A

£8640

C

£7527

D

£11 213

E

£19 251

I. A and B

```
    9 6 1 1
  - 8 6 4 0
  _____
```

Copy and complete.

II.
```
    1 2 6 0 4
  -   9 1 5 6
```

II.
```
    1 2 6 0 4
  -   9 1 5 6
  _____
```

12
```
    1 3 8 1 1
  - 1 1 4 6 7
  _____
```

13
```
    1 0 4 1 8
  -   7 5 2 6
  _____
```

14
```
    1 5 7 2 4
  - 1 3 6 3 5
  _____
```

15
```
    1 4 2 4 9
  -   8 3 5 6
  _____
```

16
```
    1 8 9 4 2
  -   9 7 5 3
  _____
```

17
```
    1 7 8 8 1
  - 1 5 9 1 5
  _____
```

18
```
    1 4 4 3 1
  -   8 5 6 2
  _____
```

19
```
    1 3 8 0 6
  -   7 6 2 4
  _____
```

33

> Write how many children in each crowd.

Manchester United

1

44 750 total
35 800 adults

I.
```
  4 4 7 5 0
- 3 5 8 0 0
```
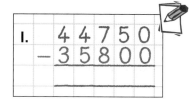

2 **Aston Villa**

29 343 total
22 557 adults

3 **Blackburn Rovers**

21 653 total
17 584 adults

4 **Leeds United**

28 334 total
21 447 adults

5 **Derby County**

26 590 total
21 672 adults

6 **Celtic**

31 163 total
23 683 adults

7 **Sheffield Wednesday**

32 101 total
25 680 adults

8 **Liverpool**

39 707 total
29 788 adults

9 **Leicester City**

20 628 total
15 883 adults

10 **Arsenal**

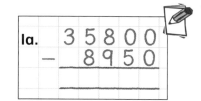

28 232 total
19 762 adults

> For each crowd, write the difference between the numbers of adults and children.

1a.
```
  3 5 8 0 0
-   8 9 5 0
```

Taking away

> Write the difference between each cheque and the amount in the safe.

1

£24 340

1.	4	3	2	2	2
–	2	4	3	4	0
£					

2

£28 675

3

£16 450

4

£39 451

5

£29 994

6

£11 784

7

£36 427

£43 222

8

£39 889

9

£40 666

10

£32 777

> Copy and complete.

11
```
  1 3 4 2 3
-   7 8 9 6
_____

_____
```

II.	1	3	4	2	3
–		7	8	9	6

12
```
  7 8 2 4 3
- 5 0 5 6 8
_____

```

13
```
  1 7 4 3 1
-   4 4 4 4
_____

```

14
```
  2 1 7 4 6
-   9 4 8 7
_____

```

15
```
  1 9 0 4 0 1
-   1 7 6 7 4
_____

```

16
```
  1 7 3 6 2 3
-   2 8 7 8 2
_____

```

17
```
  1 8 5 2 4 6
-   7 3 8 9 7
_____

```

18
```
  1 6 3 8 1 4
-   5 7 7 2 5
_____

```

19
```
  1 5 6 6 2 8
-   7 5 7 3 4
_____

```

Write how far each rocket is from the Moon.

1

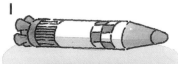

46 968 miles from Earth

```
 1.    2 3 8 8 5 7
     −   4 6 9 6 8
     _____
```

Earth to Moon is 238 857 miles.

2

39 749 miles from Earth

3
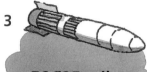

56 925 miles from Earth

4

139 968 miles from Earth

5

74 865 miles from Earth

6

204 789 miles from Earth

7

158 918 miles from Earth

8

219 868 miles from Earth

Copy and complete.

```
9      1 3 2 4 2 3
     −   1 8 7 4 8
     _____
```

```
 9.    1 3 2 4 2 3
     −   1 8 7 4 8
     _____
```

```
10    6 4 2 0 8
    −   8 6 7 5
    _____
```

```
11    1 7 4 6 1 0 8
    −     8 7 8 7 9
    _____
```

```
12    9 3 4 2 1 1
    −   1 9 8 6 8
    _____
```

```
13    4 7 0 2
    − 1 0 1 9
    _____
```

```
14    9 7 0 2 2
    −   9 8 9 5
    _____
```

```
15    8 7 6 4 1 3
    −   6 5 6 2 8
    _____
```

```
16    1 9 9 2 8 4
    −   7 6 5 7 6
    _____
```

```
17    2 8 1 2 0 7
    −   5 3 4 1 6
    _____
```

Dividing

> Copy and complete.

I. $5\overline{)60}$

I. $5\overline{)6\,0}$ = 12

2   $4\overline{)80}$ 3 $3\overline{)63}$ 4 $5\overline{)95}$ 5 $2\overline{)42}$ 6 $5\overline{)75}$

7   $3\overline{)36}$ 8 $5\overline{)90}$ 9 $2\overline{)28}$ 10 $5\overline{)100}$ II $4\overline{)48}$

12 $3\overline{)42}$ 13 $4\overline{)84}$ 14 $3\overline{)96}$ 15 $5\overline{)85}$ 16 $4\overline{)60}$

> Write how many children in each team.

17   **45 children in 3 teams**

17. $3\overline{)4\,5}$ = 15

18   **64 children in 4 teams**

19   **72 children in 4 teams**

20   **81 children in 3 teams**

21   **78 children in 6 teams**

22   **92 children in 2 teams**

23   **54 children in 3 teams**

24   **68 children in 4 teams**

25   **78 children in 3 teams**

26   **96 children in 4 teams**

Dividing

> There are 7 sticks of gum in a pack.

> Each child has 1 stick.

> How many packs for each group?

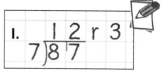

1.
$$7\overline{)8\,7} = 1\,2 \; r\,3$$

1 87 children

2 93 children

3 81 children
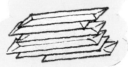

4 95 children

5 85 children
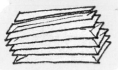

6 97 children

7 82 children

8 78 children

> There are 4 photos on a page.

> How many pages for each set?

9.
$$4\overline{)9\,{}^1 8} = 2\,4 \; r\,2$$

9 98 photos

10 71 photos

11 67 photos

12 59 photos

13 61 photos

14 85 photos

15 73 photos

16 55 photos

> Complete these divisions.

17 $64 \div 3$

17.
$$3\overline{)6\,4} = 2\,1 \; r\,1$$

18 $59 \div 2$

19 $71 \div 5$

20 $82 \div 3$

21 $74 \div 5$

22 $87 \div 3$

23 $67 \div 4$

24 $89 \div 5$

25 $52 \div 3$

Dividing

Copy and complete.

1   3⟌135

I.
```
        4 5
3⟌1 3¹5
```

2   3⟌168   3   3⟌465   4   3⟌369   5   3⟌432   6   3⟌861

7   3⟌762   8   3⟌567   9   3⟌651   10   3⟌441   11   3⟌642

Each amount is divided among 5 friends.

How much is left over?

12.
```
     1 4 8 r 3
5⟌7 ²4 ⁴3
£ 3  is left over
```

12   £743

13   £497

14   £424

15   £376

16   £147

17   £573

18   £846

19   £648

20   £168

21   £237

22   £861

23   £282

Dividing

There are 9 beads on a bracelet. How many are left over?

1.
```
      1 3 r 2
  9 )1 1 ²9
```

1 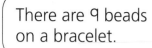 119 beads

2 208 beads

3 191 beads

4 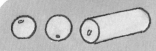 217 beads

5  171 beads

6 220 beads

7 379 beads

8 460 beads

9 517 beads

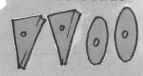

There are 6 beads on an earring. How many are left over?

10.
```
      1 7 r 2
  6 )1 0 ⁴4
```

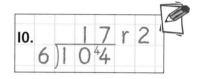

10 104 beads

11 203 beads

12 136 beads

13 119 beads

14 147 beads

15 256 beads

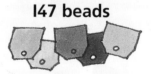

16 316 beads

17 732 beads

18 860 beads

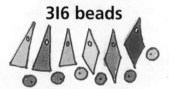
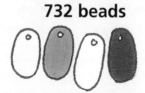
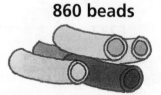

Dividing

There are 7 stickers in a pack. | How many are left over?

$$1. \quad 7\overline{)9^27}\ \ {}^{1\ 3\ r\ 6}$$

1 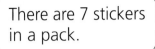 97 stickers

2 115 stickers

3 296 stickers

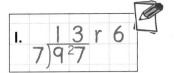

4 156 stickers

5 189 stickers

6 227 stickers

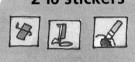

7 305 stickers

8 353 stickers

9 431 stickers

There are 8 marbles in a bag. | How many are left over?

$$10. \quad 8\overline{)2\ 0^47}\ \ {}^{2\ 5\ r\ 7}$$

10 207 marbles

11 104 marbles

12 219 marbles

13 117 marbles

14 333 marbles

15 197 marbles

16 257 marbles

17 339 marbles

18 416 marbles

Dividing

The children on the train sit in fours.

How many are left over?

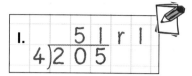

1.
$$4\overline{)205} \quad = 51\ r\ 1$$

1 **205 children**

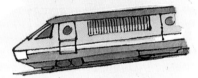

2 **337 children**

3 **217 children**

4 **251 children**

5 **341 children**

6 **278 children**

7 **457 children**

8 **310 children**

9 **267 children**

10 **519 children**

11 **634 children**

12 **561 children**

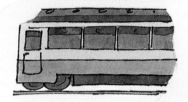

Explore

Divide 100 by 9.

Divide 200 by 9.

Divide 300 by 9.

Continue for 400, 500, …

Write about any patterns.

Dividing

Copy and complete.

1 $210 \div 30 =$

1. $2\,1\,0 \div 3\,0$
   $\rightarrow 2\,1 \div 3 = 7$

2 $330 \div 30 =$ **3** $420 \div 30 =$ **4** $180 \div 30 =$ **5** $300 \div 30 =$

6 $360 \div 30 =$ **7** $450 \div 30 =$ **8** $390 \div 30 =$ **9** $480 \div 30 =$

How many £20 notes would you need to buy each of these?

10 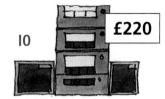 £220

10. $2\,2\,0 \div 2\,0$
    $\rightarrow 2\,2 \div 2 = 1\,1$

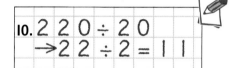

11  £180   **12**  £160   **13**  £240   **14** 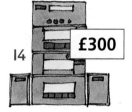 £300

15 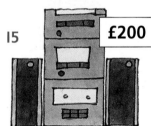 £200   **16**  £140   **17** 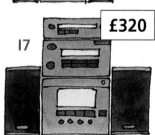 £320   **18**  £260

How many £50 notes would you need to buy each of these?

19  £400

19. $4\,0\,0 \div 5\,0$
    $\rightarrow 4\,0 \div 5 = 8$

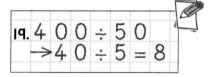

20 £250   **21** £200   **22** £350   **23** £450

24 £150   **25** £550   **26**  £500   **27**  £100

Dividing

How many minutes has each child been swimming?

1 **360 seconds**

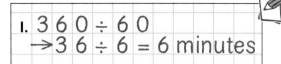

1. 3 6 0 ÷ 6 0
   → 3 6 ÷ 6 = 6 minutes

2 **480 seconds**

3 **600 seconds**

4 **240 seconds**

5 **540 seconds**

6 **120 seconds**

7 **420 seconds**

8 **180 seconds**

9 **300 seconds**

10 **660 seconds**

How many right-angles in each turn?

11 **720°**

II. 7 2 0 ÷ 9 0
   → 7 2 ÷ 9 = 8

12 **180°**

13 **360°**

14 **450°**

15 **810°**

16 **270°**

17 **630°**

18 **900°**

19 **540°**

Dividing

> Copy and complete.

1 $480 \div 80 =$

```
1. 4 8 0 ÷ 8 0
   → 4 8 ÷ 8 = 6
```

2 $210 \div 70 =$ **3** $320 \div 80 =$ **4** $350 \div 70 =$

5 $420 \div 70 =$ **6** $640 \div 80 =$ **7** $490 \div 70$

8 $240 \div 80 =$ **9** $560 \div 70 =$ **10** $720 \div 80 =$

11 $140 \div 70 =$ **12** $280 \div 70 =$ **13** $160 \div 80 =$

> Each coach carries 40 people.

> How many coaches are needed for each group?

```
14. 2 4 0 ÷ 4 0
    → 2 4 ÷ 4 = 6
```

14   240 people

15   440 people

16   280 people

17   320 people

18   480 people

19   160 people

20   560 people

21   520 people

22   360 people

Dividing

Write the missing numbers.

1   $120 \div$ 🌼 $= 6$

I. $120 \div 20 = 6$

2   $150 \div$ 🌼 $= 5$

3   $630 \div$ 🌼 $= 9$

4   $400 \div$ 🌼 $= 5$

5   $120 \div$ 🌼 $= 4$

6   🌼 $\div 40 = 3$

7   $90 \div$ 🌼 $= 3$

8   $560 \div$ 🌼 $= 7$

9   🌼 $\div 50 = 6$

10   🌼 $\div 40 = 5$

Copy and complete.

11   $4000 \div 400 =$

II. $4000 \div 400$
$\rightarrow 400 \div 40 = 10$

12   $3600 \div 60 =$

13   $4500 \div 500 =$

14   $1500 \div 30 =$

15   $3200 \div 400 =$

16   $4200 \div 20 =$

17   $6300 \div 90 =$

18   $2100 \div 700 =$

19   $2600 \div 200 =$

20   $2400 \div 300 =$

 ## Explore

Divide 80 000 by 20, 200 and 2000.

Divide 80 000 by 40, 400 and 4000.

Can you see a pattern?

Invent some more divisions that follow a similar pattern.

Solving problems

> Solve each problem.

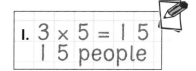

1. 3 × 5 = 15
   15 people

1

| 5 people in a car. |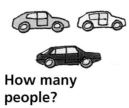
How many people? |

2

| Car wash £5·50. | 2 cars.
How much money? |

3

| Raffle tickets
1 for 50p
3 for £1 |
How many for £4·50? |

4

| David
Last year 1·26 m
This year 1·32 m | John
Last year 1·19 m
This year 1·27 m
———
Has John grown more than David? |

5

 | Can you watch both videos before 10:00?

6

| 450 ml of medicine each day.  | 5 doses a day.
How much in each dose? |

7

 £10 each from Auntie Jo. |  £7·50 between us from Uncle Sam. | Share the money and buy a video for £15·98.

How much left each?

> Make up your own stories to solve these problems.

8 £25 − £10·50 − £4·75 =

9 90 minutes after 12:15

10 120 metres ÷ 3 =

Solving problems

> Solve each problem.

1

| Tom has a job washing windows.  | He gets £2·50 for each house.  | He washes 5 houses. | He buys a sandwich for £1·25 and a drink for 65p. | How much does he have left? |

2

| Bill, Sue, Sally and Zac all start the race together.  | Bill finishes at 4:12. Sue finishes at 4:27.  | Sally finishes at 4:17. Zac finishes at 4:31. | Write the race times and the differences in time.  | Write the race order.  |

3

| Renu and Jo each have £10.  | First they go on the Dodgems.  £3 a car | Then they have two turns each at the Big Wheel. £2 each | Then they go in the Ghost House.  50p each | How many turns can they have on the Water Chute?  £2·50 each |

4

| Ben and Amy are planning a party.  | They invite 25 friends.  | 21 accept. 16 want to bring a friend. | On the day 8 people have a cold and can't come. | How many people are at the party?  |

> Make up your own real-life problem. Give it to someone else to solve.

Solving problems

> Solve each problem.

1   (2 + 8) × 10 =

```
1. 2 + 8 = 1 0
   1 0 × 1 0 = 1 0 0
```

2   (5 + 7) × 3 =

3   (12 – 3) ÷ 3 =

> Always do the part in brackets first.

4   (4 × 2) + 26 =

5   (8 + 2) × 22 =

6   (34 – 8) × 5 =

7   10 × (16 + 4) =

8   (2 × 3) + 24 =

9   (32 – 16) × 2 =

10   (4 + 4) × 4 =

11   (12 + 8) × 4 =

12   17 – (2 × 8) =

13   29 + (3 × 8) =

14   (16 ÷ 8) × 44 =

15   (32 ÷ 4) – 4 =

16   (10 × 9) – 9 =

17   (2 + 6) × (3 + 2) =

> Solve each problem.

18 Jane bought 4 boxes of sweets. She ate 6 sweets and had 14 left. How many sweets in each box?

19 Sam had 10 packs of stickers. He gave away 8 stickers and had 32 left. How many stickers in each pack?

20 Craig has £20. He buys 2 lights and a bell for his bike. The bell is £7. He has £2 left. How much is each light?

21 Pearl cycles to her friend's house. They then cycle 4 miles to the beach. Later they cycle back. Pearl cycles home. She cycled 15 miles in total. How far is it to her friend's house?

22 Amit has lots of new pencils. He gives each of eight friends three pencils. He has six left. How many pencils did he start with?

Multiplying decimals

> Each fence has 10 pieces.

> Write the total length of each fence.

I. $10 \times 3 \cdot 8 = 38\,m$

1

3·8 m

2

4·4 m

3

1·5 m

4

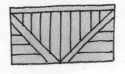

3·5 m

5

1·2 m

6

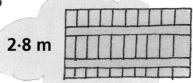

2·8 m

7

3·1 m

8

0·9 m

9

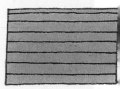

0·7 m

10

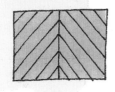

4·1 m

11

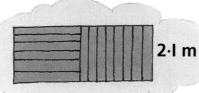

2·1 m

12

3·7 m

> Copy and complete.

13 $10 \times 2 \cdot 7 =$

13. $10 \times 2 \cdot 7 = 27$

14 $10 \times 1 \cdot 3 =$

15 $10 \times 9 \cdot 5 =$

16 $10 \times 0 \cdot 8 =$

17 $10 \times 3 \cdot 4 =$

18 $10 \times 13 \cdot 4 =$

19 $10 \times 21 \cdot 3 =$

20 $10 \times 6 \cdot 0 =$

21 $10 \times 19 \cdot 7 =$

22 $10 \times 43 \cdot 8 =$

23 $10 \times 4 \cdot 0 =$

24 $10 \times 12 \cdot 5 =$

25 $10 \times 61 \cdot 4 =$

Multiplying decimals

> Write the total distance each child travels to and from school in a week.

1
4·7 km

| 1. | 1 | 0 | × | 4 | · | 7 | = | 4 | 7 | km |

2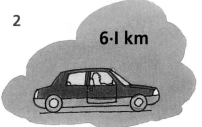
6·1 km

3
1·9 km

4
2·8 km

5
3·5 km

6
16·3 km

7
7·5 km

8
0·8 km

9
11·9 km

10
12 km

> Multiply each number by 10.

11 **6·32**

| 11. | 1 | 0 | × | 6 | · | 3 | 2 | = | 6 | 3 | · | 2 |

12 **4·13**

13 **2·8**

14 **7**

15 **3·5**

16 **4·67**

17 **18·3**

18 **11·58**

19 **1·09**

20 **15·2**

21 **7·9**

51

Multiplying decimals

Copy and complete.

1 10 × 1·74 =

1. | 10 × 1·74 = 17·4

2 10 × 2·31 =

3 10 × 1·86=

4 10 × 1·92 =

5 10 × 3·16 =

6 10 × 2·73 =

7 10 × 0·93 =

8 10 × 10·8 =

9 10 × 2·75 =

10 10 × 2·09 =

A warehouse buys 10 of each item.

Write the total cost.

11. | 10 × 3·26 = £32·60

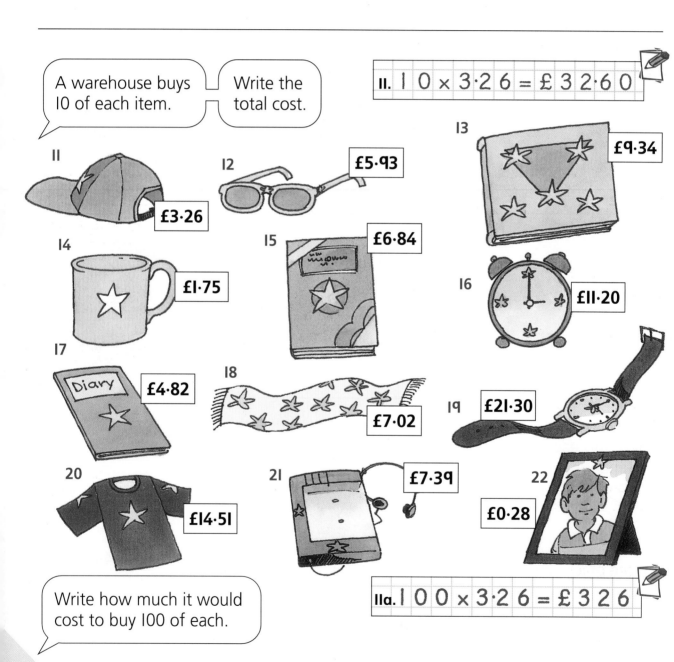

11 £3·26

12 £5·93

13 £9·34

14 £1·75

15 £6·84

16 £11·20

17 £4·82

18 £7·02

19 £21·30

20 £14·51

21 £7·39

22 £0·28

Write how much it would cost to buy 100 of each.

11a. | 100 × 3·26 = £326

52

Multiplying decimals

> Write the missing numbers.

1 ⬤ × 2·3 = 230

1. | 1 0 0 × 2·3 = 2 3 0

2   10 × ⬤ = 15

3   10 × ⬤ = 34

4   100 × ⬤ = 760

5   100 × ⬤ = 480

6   ⬤ × 31·2 = 312

7   ⬤ × 4·23 = 423

8   100 × ⬤ = 675

9   10 × ⬤ = 80·9

10   100 × ⬤ = 938

11   ⬤ × 16·45 = 1645

12   10 × ⬤ = 93·8

13   100 × ⬤ = 895

14   ⬤ × 67 = 670

15   10 × ⬤ = 73

16   100 × ⬤ = 21

> Multiply each red number by each blue number.

17. | 1 0 × 4·8 = 4 8

1000

10

100

4·8

2·01

3·96

Explore

Multiply 2·1 by 10, 100, 1000, 20, 200.

Explore quick ways of multiplying other decimal numbers by 10, 100, 1000, 20 and 200.

How quickly can you say the answers, without writing?

Multiplying decimals

> Complete these multiplications.

1   5 × 2·4

I.	(1 0)
	2·4
×	5
	2·0
	1 0·0
	1 2·0

2   3 × 4·3   3   6 × 3·4   4   3 × 7·2

5   4 × 6·8   6   6 × 1·9   7   3 × 3·4

8   4 × 1·4   9   5 × 3·7   10   4 × 2·6   11   6 × 5·4

12   3 × 4·9   13   6 × 2·8   14   4 × 1·9   15   3 × 3·7

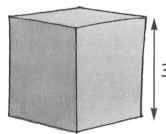
3·2 cm

1·9 cm

3·5 cm
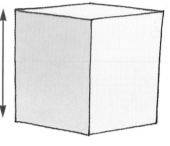

2·7 cm

2·5 cm

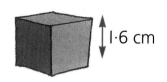
1·6 cm

> Write the heights of towers built with these cubes.

16   3 blue

16.	(9 cm)
	3·2
×	3
	·6
	9·0
	9·6 cm

17   4 red   18   6 yellow   19   5 pink

20   3 orange   21   2 brown   22   3 yellow

23   2 red   24   3 pink   25   4 brown   26   5 blue

27   6 orange   28   5 brown   29   6 red   30   4 orange

Multiplying decimals

 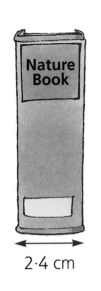  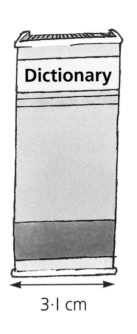 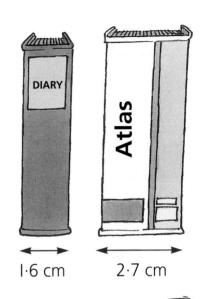

| QUIZ BOOK | Nature Book | Annual | Dictionary | DIARY | Atlas |

| 1·3 cm | 2·4 cm | 1·8 cm | 3·1 cm | 1·6 cm | 2·7 cm |

Write the total width of:

I   5 dictionaries

```
I.      I 5 cm
        3·I
    ×     5
         ·5
      I 5·0
      I 5·5 cm
```

2   4 atlases

3   3 annuals

4   2 quiz books

5   6 nature books

6   4 diaries

7   3 atlases

8   5 annuals

9   6 quiz books

10   5 diaries

II   8 nature books

12   6 atlases

13   7 diaries

14   6 annuals

15   7 dictionaries

Complete these multiplications.

16   3 × 2·6

17   4 × 1·8

18   2 × 3·8

19   4 × 5·6

20   6 × 3·4

21   7 × 1·9

22   8 × 2·5

23   9 × 3·7

24   4 × 6·3

25   3 × 11·2

26   2 × 15·7

These are regular polygons. The sides of each are the same length.

Write the perimeter of each polygon.

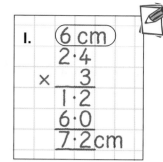

I. 6 cm
    2·4
×   3
    1·2
    6·0
    7·2 cm

1 2·4 cm

2 3·2 cm

3 1·7 cm

4 2·3 cm

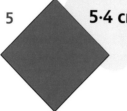

5 5·4 cm

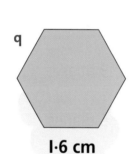

6 2·7 cm

7 4·3 cm

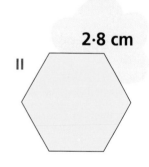

8 6·4 cm

9 1·6 cm

10 3·5 cm

11 2·8 cm

Complete these multiplications.

12 4 × 5·3

13 5 × 16·2

14 3 × 12·7

15 4 × 15·4

16 7 × 11·8

17 8 × 12·6

18 3 × 15·2

19 5 × 10·7

20 4 × 21·3

21 6 × 13·8

22 7 × 14·3

Multiplying decimals

Copy and complete the table for each multiplication machine.

I.

in	1·2	2·3	3·5		
out	3·6				

in	1·2	2·3	3·5	7·5	8·4
out					

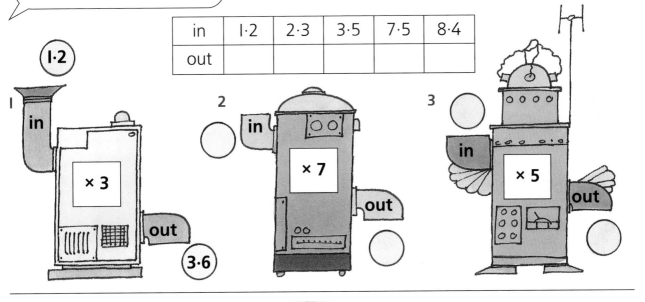

1 in × 3 out (1·2) → (3·6)

2 in × 7 out

3 in × 5 out

Write the weight of 6 of each.

4 RHINO DINO 3·2 kg

4.
```
  1 8 kg
    3·2
×     6
    1·2
  1 8·0
  1 9·2 kg
```

5 JUMBO CHUNKS 1·9 kg

6 Tiger Treats 4·3 kg

7 Dolphin Delights 5·1 kg

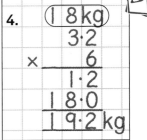

8 WHALE POOD 2·6 kg

9 LIONS SHARE 3·7 kg

10 Cheese Cheetah 4·6 kg

11 Picky Panther 5·4 kg

Explore

Use number cards 2, 3, 4, 5.

Choose three to make a decimal multiplication.

What is the nearest answer you can make to 10, 12, 14, 16, 18, 20?

3 **4**

5

```
  3·4
×   5
  2·0
  1 5
  1 7·0
```

Dividing

Copy and complete.

1   3·7 × 10 =
       37 ÷ 10 =

1. 3·7 × 1 0 = 3 7
    37 ÷ 1 0 = 3·7

2   9·2 × 10 =
     92 ÷ 10 =

3   6·2 × 10 =
     62 ÷ 10 =

4   8·7 × 10 =
     87 ÷ 10 =

5   7·5 × 10 =
     75 ÷ 10 =

6   3·9 × 10 =
     39 ÷ 10 =

7   6·3 × 10 =
     63 ÷ 10 =

Copy and complete.

8   38 ÷ 10 =

8. 3 8 ÷ 1 0 = 3·8

9   43 ÷ 10 =

10   29 ÷ 10 =

11   49 ÷ 10 =

12   76 ÷ 10 =

13   32 ÷ 10 =

14   15 ÷ 10 =

15   99 ÷ 10 =

16   66 ÷ 10 =

17   90 ÷ 10 =

Write each measurement in centimetres.

18

26 mm

18. 2 6 ÷ 1 0 = 2·6 cm

19
95 mm

20
44 mm

21
77 mm

22
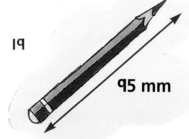
80 mm

23

61 mm

24

98 mm

Dividing

Divide each amount by 10.

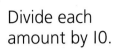

£58

I. 5 8 ÷ 1 0 = 5·8
   £ 5·8 0

2 £69

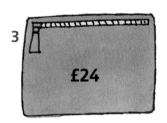

3 £24

4 £14

5 £98

6 £36

7 £72

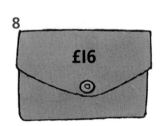

8 £16

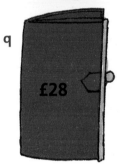

9 £28

Here are the distances each person travels to and from work in a week.

Write the distance of one journey.

10. 4 2 ÷ 1 0 = 4·2 km

10 42 km

11 18 km

12 23 km

13 8 km

14 37 km

15 28 km

16 6 km

17 11 km

18 5 km

19 21 km

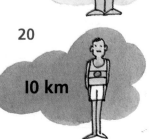

20 10 km

21 100 km

Dividing

> Copy and complete.

1 341 ÷ 100 =

I. 341 ÷ 100 = 3·41

2 621 ÷ 100 =

3 107 ÷ 100 =

4 505 ÷ 100 =

5 660 ÷ 100 =

6 999 ÷ 100 =

7 330 ÷ 100 =

8 190 ÷ 100 =

9 202 ÷ 100 =

10 111 ÷ 100 =

> Write each amount in pounds.

II. 248 ÷ 100 = £2·48

11 248p

12 144p

13 399p

14 919p

15 707p

16 818p

17 601p

18 702p

19 350p

20 208p

21 611p

22 909p

23 220p

Dividing

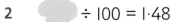 Write the missing numbers.

1   $156 ÷$ $= 15·6$

1. $156 ÷ 10 = 15·6$

2   ◯ $÷ 100 = 1·48$

3   $246 ÷$ ◯ $= 24·6$

4   $391 ÷$ ◯ $= 3·91$

5   ◯ $÷ 10 = 1·48$

6   ◯ $÷ 100 = 5·07$

7   $786 ÷$ ◯ $= 78·6$

8   $841 ÷$ ◯ $= 8·41$

9   ◯ $÷ 100 = 2·11$

10 $929 ÷$ ◯ $= 92·9$

11 $735 ÷$ ◯ $= 7·35$

12 ◯ $÷ 10 = 15·5$

13 $232 ÷$ ◯ $= 2·32$

Copy and complete the table for the dividing machine.

in	34·6	29·8	17·6
out	3·4 6		

in	34·6	29·8	17·6	3·4	21·5	16·4				42·3
out							9·6	4·51	3·28	

34·6 in   ÷ 10   out **3·46**

 Explore

Find 5 objects and measure them in centimetres.

Write each length in metres.

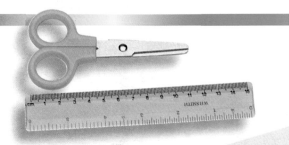

Dividing decimals

Copy and complete.

1 $4\overline{)9{\cdot}2}$

1. $\begin{array}{r} 2{\cdot}3 \\ 4\overline{)9{\cdot}2} \end{array}$

2 $5\overline{)12{\cdot}5}$ 3 $3\overline{)13{\cdot}2}$ 4 $2\overline{)7{\cdot}2}$ 5 $4\overline{)17{\cdot}6}$

6 $5\overline{)34{\cdot}5}$ 7 $3\overline{)22{\cdot}8}$ 8 $6\overline{)13{\cdot}8}$ 9 $4\overline{)46{\cdot}4}$

10 $2\overline{)27{\cdot}6}$ 11 $6\overline{)37{\cdot}8}$ 12 $9\overline{)36{\cdot}9}$ 13 $8\overline{)17{\cdot}6}$

Write the length of one side of each square picture.

14 **perimeter, 8·4 m**

14. $\begin{array}{r} 2{\cdot}1 \text{ m} \\ 4\overline{)8{\cdot}4} \end{array}$

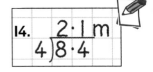

15 **perimeter, 15·2 m**

16 **perimeter, 17·6 m**

17 **perimeter, 27·2 m**

18 **perimeter, 11·6 m**

19 **perimeter, 25·6 m**

20 **perimeter, 31·2 m**

21 **perimeter, 29·6 m**

22 **perimeter, 18·4 m**

23 **perimeter, 14·4 m**

Dividing decimals

Here are the total hours each person worked during 5 days.

Write the average time each worked per day.

1.
```
     7·3 hours
5)3 6·5
```

1 36·5 hours

2 40·5 hours

3 34·5 hours

4 38·5 hours

5 35·5 hours

6 41·5 hours

7 35 hours

8 37·5 hours

Write the average weight of each fruit.

9 2·4 kg

9.
```
   0·4 kg
6)2·4
```

10 1·8 kg

11 1·6 kg

12 2·8 kg
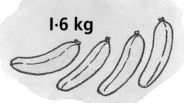

13 1·2 kg

14 2·0 kg
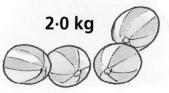

15 2·1 kg
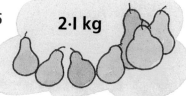

16 3·5 kg

17 1·2 kg

18 1·6 kg
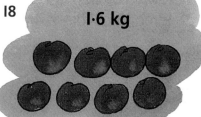

Dividing decimals

Write the missing numbers.

1
$$3\overline{)\cdot} = 1\cdot6$$

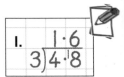

1.
$$3\overline{)4\cdot8} = 1\cdot6$$

2
$$4\overline{)\cdot} = 2\cdot4$$

3
$$5\overline{)\cdot} = 1\cdot5$$

4
$$\overline{)4\cdot8} = 2\cdot4$$

5
$$\overline{)6\cdot9} = 2\cdot3$$

6
$$\overline{)5\cdot6} = 2\cdot8$$

7
$$\overline{)7\cdot2} = 2\cdot4$$

8
$$4\overline{)\cdot} = 1\cdot9$$

9
$$6\overline{)\cdot} = 1\cdot3$$

Divide each amount equally among the children.

10 £7·80

10.
$$3\overline{)7\cdot8} = 2\cdot6$$
£2·60 each

11 £18·40

12 £10·80

13 £22·50

14 £13·80

15 £63·20

16 £54·60

Explore

Try dividing £19·20 equally among 2 children, 3 children, 4 children, …

How much does each child get?